I0029624

MIGRATION AND DEVELOPMENT IN MOZAMBIQUE: POVERTY, INEQUALITY AND SURVIVAL

FION DE VLETTER

SERIES EDITOR:
PROF. JONATHAN CRUSH

SOUTHERN AFRICAN MIGRATION PROJECT
2006

Published by Idasa, 6 Spin Street, Church Square, Cape Town, 8001, and Southern African Research Centre, Queen's University, Canada.

Copyright Southern African Migration Project (SAMP) 2006
ISBN 1-920118-10-1

First published 2006
Design by Bronwen Müller
Typeset in Goudy

All rights reserved. No part of this publication may be reproduced or transmitted, in any form or by any means, without prior permission from the publishers.
Bound and printed by Logo Print, Cape Town

CONTENTS	PAGE

TABLES	PAGE

EXECUTIVE SUMMARY

Despite Mozambique's economic growth rate being one of the highest in Africa over the past few years, much of the growth is linked to the development of highly capital intensive "mega" projects with limited absorption of unskilled workers. The urban informal sector which has hitherto absorbed considerable numbers of the unemployed has become less attractive for the rural labour surpluses as increasing competition makes economic survival more difficult. Such limitations within the domestic economy, recently exacerbated by the current drought in the South, have forced many rural households to seek employment in South Africa. Although external migration to South Africa is the preferred employment option for many Mozambicans, it represents the option of last resort for many others simply because of the limited employment absorption capacity of Mozambique's formal economy.

The South African mines are the traditional destination of male Mozambican labour migrants. The number of migrants has remained relatively consistent over the last decade despite major downsizing in the industry as a whole. Mozambicans now make up 25% of the gold-mine workforce (up from 10% in 1990). Mozambican miners may collectively be seen as a wage elite. Households with several generations of miners are likely to have built up assets and a home-based production capacity that would put them well above the economic status of other households with a more recent involvement in mine-migration. Households with miners with greater skills, longer service or with more than one miner, may have relatively high earnings. However, a significant proportion of sending households could be considered to be poor. Differentiation between households is even more pronounced when looked at across the entire range of migrant-sending households.

Rural Southern Mozambique, an area relatively bereft of resources and traditionally less productive agriculturally than other regions of Mozambique (due to poorer soils and erratic weather patterns) is now more developed and better off (at least in terms of average income and levels of wealth) than other rural areas. The pool of economic assets of the average rural household in the South is far greater than for other regions. This difference is largely attributable to labour migration and the transfer of significant volumes of remittances. There is, however, much evidence to suggest that many migrant households remain poor, having low levels of agricultural production and being highly dependent on relatively low levels of wage transfers.

Especially since the abolition of apartheid, employment opportunities for Mozambicans in South Africa have become much more varied, leading to á much higher degree of household differentiation than prevailed before 1990. In South Africa, employment is available for almost anyone willing to risk the consequences of unauthorized entry and prepared to be exploited, meaning that the remittances or accumulated wages brought home are likely to be minimal. Although migrant worker households are often better off than non-migrant supplying households, significant numbers of such households are still vulnerable to poverty. These households are usually deficit agricultural producers, being largely dependent on migrant remittances. In turn, with the increasingly harsh attitude to unskilled undocumented migrants in South Africa, their employment situation has become less and less secure.

This paper undertakes an inter-regional analysis of the South, Centre and North of Mozambique, demonstrating clear developmental differences attributed to many years of remittances channeled to the mainly rural areas of Southern Mozambique. This is followed by an analysis of the results of SAMP's Migration and Remittances Survey (MARS) conducted in Southern Mozambique in 2004 which provides useful insights into the disparity of wealth and well-being among migrant-sending households.

Although the overall economic impact of migrant labour has been positive in the South of Mozambique, because the nature of migration has changed so significantly over the last 15 years (i.e. the eclipsing of mine migration and increasing numbers of young Mozambican men chasing a limited number of jobs), it is likely that, in the coming years, the economic impact of migrant labour work in South Africa may diminish quite substantially as the amounts of wages remitted are reduced (due to lower earnings) and the mechanisms available for doing so are much more limited than for miners and workers in other, more privileged, wage sectors.

INTRODUCTION

Southern Mozambique has been a significant labour exporting area for more than 150 years.[1] Apart from migration occurring from Tete Province to Southern Rhodesia in the early 1900s, the rest of Mozambique supplied almost no external labour migrants and experienced comparatively little internal labour migration. Such a regional dichotomy allows for interesting comparisons, especially in relation to the impact of migration on household accumulation and wealth. In the 1980s, household differentiation was clearly evident in Southern Mozambique due largely to the fairly significant wage differentials between relatively skilled and unskilled mineworkers.[2] Although many migrant-sending households clearly benefited from migration, the majority of migrant-sending households remained impoverished and became wage-dependent as their capacity to produce subsistence crops diminished. External work opportunities and conditions for migrants, especially since the abolition of apartheid, have become much more varied, leading to a much higher degree of household differentiation than prevailed from the mid-1800s to 1990.[3]

This paper attempts to demonstrate that rural Southern Mozambique, an area relatively bereft of resources and traditionally less productive agriculturally than other regions of Mozambique (due to poorer soils and erratic weather patterns) is now more developed and better off (at least in terms of average income and levels of wealth) than other rural areas. This difference is largely attributed to labour migration and the transfer of significant volumes of remittances.

Although migrant worker households are often seen as better off than non-migrant supplying households, there are, indeed, significant numbers of such households that are vulnerable to poverty. These households are usually deficit agricultural producers, being largely dependent on migrant remittances. In turn, with the increasingly harsh position on unskilled irregular migrants in South Africa, their employment situation has become less and less secure.[4] Although external migration is the preferred employment option for many Mozambicans, it represents the option of last resort for many others simply because of the limited employment absorption capacity Mozambique's formal economy. In South Africa, employment is available for almost anyone willing to risk the consequences of illegal entry and prepared to be exploited, meaning that the remittances or accumulated wages brought home are likely to be minimal.

This paper undertakes an inter-regional analysis (based on the results of a national survey of some 4,000 rural households) of the South, Centre and North of Mozambique, demonstrating clear developmental differences attributable to many years of remittances channeled to the mainly rural areas of southern Mozambique. This is then complemented by an analysis of the results of SAMP's Migration and Remittance Survey (MARS) conducted in Southern Mozambique in 2004 which provides useful insights into the disparity of wealth and well-being among migrant-sending households.

METHODOLOGY

This study draws mainly from the results of two surveys: the ANE/Austral Survey of Rural Households (1999-2001) and the SAMP Migration and Remittances Survey (MARS) (2004) described below. Supporting data was drawn from the SAMP Survey of Mozambican Miners (1996). The rural household study is used because it incorporated detailed questions on migrant labour and looked at a broad range of variables to determine household wealth which were felt to be more adequate in measuring the developmental impact of remittances. The results of the recent Migrant and Remittances Survey (MARS) provide important new revelations on migrant remittance patterns which help us better understand the influence of migration on development and household differentiation. Details of the three surveys are provided below.

ANE/AUSTRAL SURVEY OF RURAL HOUSEHOLDS (1999-2001)

The National Roads Administration (ANE) in collaboration with the consulting company Austral Consultants conducted a comprehensive rural household survey covering all regions of Mozambique along selected sections of rehabilitated secondary roads. The sample consisted of approximately 4,000 households. These households were visited annually during a period of 3 years (1999-2001) with the objective of measuring the socio-economic impact of road rehabilitation. The survey provided an excellent opportunity to collect detailed economic data for rural households including comprehensive information on migrant labour.[5] Because of the amount of information the survey was able to collect, an analysis of household wealth was possible by converting assets, income, housing conditions and investment patterns into wealth points, allowing for regional comparisons.[6] Regions were defined as follows:

- South: Provinces of Maputo, Gaza and Inhambane as well as Maputo City;
- Centre: Sofala, Manica, Zambezia and Tete;
- North: Nampula, Niassa and Cabo Delgado.

SAMP MIGRATION AND REMITTANCES SURVEY (2004)

The SADC Migration and Remittances Survey (MARS) was conducted in Botswana, Lesotho, Malawi, Mozambique, Swaziland and Zimbabwe. The survey interviewed only households with external migrants and focused on remittance patterns and migration history. The Mozambique survey was conducted in early 2004, consisting of 726 households located only in the South. The survey areas were randomly sampled and included households in rural areas and in urban areas.[7]

SAMP SURVEY OF MOZAMBICAN MINERS (1996)

An earlier survey of mineworkers was undertaken by SAMP in Mozambique.[8] The study interviewed 455 miners during the months of August and September 1996. Interviews were conducted at the Teba/Wenela depots at Ressano Garcia and Johannesburg as well as the depots of the recruiting agency Algos which recruits mine and farm labour. In addition a separate survey instrument was used for interviewing 160 miners' wives in the provinces of Inhambane, Gaza and Maputo provinces.

WAGE EMPLOYMENT AND MIGRATION PATTERNS IN RURAL MOZAMBIQUE

Wage employment for the purposes of this paper refers to full-time employment of household members. "Full-time employment" is essentially seen as the full-time pursuit of an income-generating activity that is not linked to the household economy. Significantly, this includes the growing number of members who are engaged in informal trading activities away from home. Employees are split into two main categories: commuter workers who normally sleep at their household and absentee workers who are based sufficiently far away from their household to allow for only periodic visits. Absentee workers are essentially migrant workers and these are split into two sub-groups: internal and external i.e. working within Mozambique or in a foreign country.

The ANE study found that one-quarter of all households have at least one member engaged in wage employment but the distribution of wage-worker supplying households is highly skewed. More than half (55%) of the rural households of the South have members engaged in wage employment compared with only 18% in the Centre and 7% in the North. Second, the wage employment opportunities available for the South are overwhelmingly located at a considerable distance from the households. In the North and South more than half the wage workers are employed in the same district as their households (73% and 58% respectively). Of the households with wage employees, 75% of the households of the South have absentee workers (32% for the Centre and 41% for the North). Reflecting the relative imbalance of male adults, the percentage of female-headed households with wage workers is only 42% versus 60% for male-headed households.

Of households with a wage worker, most of those in the South have more than one worker in wage employment (averaging 1.6) while almost all in the Centre and North have around one (1.1 and 1.3 respectively). Households in the South are therefore not only more dependent in terms of the proportion of households involved with migrant labour but there is also a higher degree of labour participation in wage employment by households with wage workers. Of all the wage employees, 42.5% could be considered commuter workers i.e.workers who normally sleep at the household.

Almost one-tenth (9.6%) of all households were found to have seasonal workers (usually employed according to agricultural needs) who worked an average of 5 months a year. Seasonal work opportunities were concentrated in the South and Centre (with 14.3% and 11.6% of households providing seasonal workers respectively compared with barely more than 1% in the North).

Reflecting the higher wages in South Africa (and to a certain extent wages in Maputo), the ANE survey found in 2001 that more than two-thirds (67.6%) of the households in the South have workers earning the equivalent of more than USD 60 per month compared to only 13.7% in the Centre, while more than half of the households of the Centre claimed that wage earnings were less than US$12, or considerably less than the minimum wage.[9]

Historical and other factors have ensured that large numbers of workers from the rural South are employed outside Mozambique. The ANE study found that more than half (53%) of the wage employees coming from households of the South were working outside the country. In very sharp contrast, both the Centre and North had almost no workers migrating abroad, having, respectively, only 3% and less than 1% of their workers outside Mozambique. Despite the strong dependency on South African employment, economic development within Southern Mozambique has managed to absorb almost half (47%) of the workers coming from the rural areas of the South. Most of these workers are located outside of their districts in contrast to the large majority of workers being located near their household in the Centre and North.

The adult population for the purposes of the MARS study was defined as 20 years or older i.e. 49.1% of the household population. Of the adult population, 66% were earning an "income" of some sort and more than half (55%) of these were external migrants.[10] The survey found that that virtually all (94.1%) of the external migrants were located in South Africa and that the vast majority (93.1%) were male. Almost half (47.3%) the external migrants were found to be in the age cohort of 25-39. More than half (54.9%) of the external migrants were married, with 15% cohabitating and 26% unmarried.

Significantly, more than half (50.7%) of the migrants were sons (and in a few cases daughters) of household heads while just over a third (34.9%) of the migrants were household heads (coming from just over half of the households). More than a third (36.2%) of the total household adult population were external migrants. In 2001 the ANE survey found an average of 1.52 absentee (migrant) workers per household. In 2004, the MARS Mozambique survey found an average 1.51 external migrants per household. It would appear that almost all adult sons can be considered external migrants.[11] External migrants are generally poorly educated: only 15.2% of the external migrants have secondary education, most (70.5%) have primary education, while 8.2% have no education at all.

Almost half (46.1%) the household population were either students (22.8%) or considered to be too young to work (23.3%). Of the remaining 53.9% of the population, the biggest occupational category was farmer (27.7%), 13.9% were unemployed job seekers, 9.3% mineworkers, 4.4% trader/hawkers and 4.2% unskilled manual workers. In terms of the sectors employing migrants, minework as a single work/sectoral category still dominates (at 31.3%). The informal sector (at 11.4%) is the second most important, followed by manufacturing industry (6.4%), domestic service (3.8%) and agriculture (2.1%). A further 3.1% were self-employed business persons and 3% skilled manual workers. The remaining 30% occupy a variety of different jobs while about 7% of the total were unknown. The agricultural sector is surprisingly underrepresented since many irregular migrants entering South Africa are likely to be caught up in agricultural work in Mpumalanga Province before advancing on to other work (if at all). It may well be that agricultural work is much more dominant but that household members simply do not know where their migrant members are working.[12]

Internal migration for domestic employment from rural households in the South of Mozambique has been found to be almost as high as the rate of external migration. However, the number of household members from external migrant-sending households found working as migrants within Mozambique is very low. The MARS data shows that 19.1% of the total household population live outside of Mozambique and that only 3.7% of the household population lives away from the household in another part of Mozambique. This suggests that migrant sending households tend to either send migrants abroad or within Mozambqiue, but rarely in combination.

MIGRATION AND HOUSEHOLD WEALTH PATTERNS

Evidence collected from the ANE survey over 3 years of consecutive interviews from approximately 4,000 households, shows stark disparity between the three regions in terms of household income and assets (wealth). The South, poor in natural resources and more prone to drought and floods than the other regions, has labour migration (both external and internal) as the most important economic feature distinguishing it from the Centre and North. It is therefore hypothesized that in the absence of any other explanatory variable the significant regional differences are, in large part, attributable to the long term effects of migration. Although on average households from the South are better off in material terms compared to the rest of the country, there are many households in the South which, even with external migration, may be poorer and more vulnerable than other households in the region as both the level of remittances are low and subsistence production marginal and susceptible to unpredictable climate. Furthermore, in terms of development, household wealth may not be a good proxy as households of the South are highly dependent on employment opportunities in both South Africa and, to a lesser extent, the Maputo-Matola axis.

The data collected from both the ANE and the MARS surveys found significant demographic patterns that separated the South from the other regions but also distinguished external migrant-supplying households from other households in the South. The ANE survey found that the average household size for the South (6.38) was larger than the Centre (6.05) and in the North (5.38). Data for household size was consistent for every year of the three year study.[13]

The MARS data on external migrant-sending households clearly demonstrates the impact of external migration on household size. The average household size was 8.48, considerably higher than the average for the South found in the ANE study. This is attributable to the fact that almost 60% of the households are considered to be extended (usually having the wife of the migrant son and their children). Some 11.2% of the external migrant-sending household population is comprised of grandchildren and 4.3% of sons or daughters-in-law (the vast majority in fact being the wives of sons who have migrated). Migration does not necessarily come from large families, but in fact, creates large families by amalgamating families affected by migration (see below).

In a country like Mozambique where migrant labour is dominant in some regions, the distinction between de jure and de facto household heads is critical. In provinces such as Maputo, Gaza and Inhambane, absentee migrant husbands remain the key household decision maker, albeit not on a day to day basis. Many de jure female-headed households in the South would have been listed as household heads in most Government surveys. But in most households with absentee husbands, he was considered the household head. Only a few married females with absentee husbands were considered to be household head. The MARS survey found that only 12.3% of external migrant sending households are considered to be "female centred" (effectively de jure female headed). About a quarter (23.7%) of the households were considered to be "nuclear" and a large 59.5% were felt to be "extended". The reason for such a small percentage of de jure female-headed households is that these households have less adult labour available for migration (see discussion below).

The ANE survey found that the principal migrant sending zone (the South) has a considerably higher proportion (about one quarter) of de jure female-headed households than other regions (14.3% in the Centre and 10.9% in the North). In the South, de jure female headed households are dominated by widowed women (almost two-thirds). This partially reflects the exposure of migrant workers to dangerous work such as on the South African gold mines (in recent years, AIDS has emerged as the major risk to migrant workers with an estimated 50% of Mozambican mineworkers HIV positive).

One of the best indicators of household wealth (and some would argue welfare) in Mozambique is the material used for building residences. The building of cement houses is usually a priority for miners. The 1996 SAMP survey found that 42% of the respondents had constructed cement block housing. The ANE/Austral survey found that one of the biggest contrasts between the regions was in relation to housing: in the South almost a quarter (23.8%) of the households have constructed their principal houses with cement blocks. In the Centre this dropped to 5.4% and in the North to less than 1%. The type of roofing showed even greater variation: in the South almost two-thirds (64.6%) of the houses had non-thatch roofing (mainly zinc sheets). In the Centre 86.9% of the houses had thatch roofs and in the North almost all (98.8%).

Notable regional differences were also noted in the source of lighting and the use of river/spring water as the principal source of water.

Migration is also likely to have had a big impact on farming practices. The ANE report found some very significant regional differences. Perhaps reflecting the difference in family size as well as the poorer soil fertility, the households of the South averaged more fields (2.8) and a

Table 1: Indicators of Living Conditions			
Variable	South (%)	Centre (%)	North (%)
Cement walls	23.8	5.4	0.6
Thatch roof	34.1	86.9	98.1
Cement floor	52.0	10.1	1.9
Source of lighting – kerosene	85.9	52.8	39.6
Cooking fuel- firewood	94.9	90.5	94.0
River/spring as principal source of water	17.9	49.9	61.1
Source: ANE			

significantly larger area (3.4 Ha) cultivated. In the Centre, households cultivated an average of 2.2 fields and 2.6 Ha; in the North, 1.8 and 2.2 Ha.

Just more than half (50.6%) of the households of the South cultivate an area in excess of 2 Ha versus 31.9% in the Centre and 24.9% in the North (Table 2).

Table 2: Distribution of Cultivated Fields by Size			
Size	South	Centre	North
<1 ha	4.3	8.9	7.0
1<2 ha	45.0	59.2	68.1
2< 5 ha	37.2	26.5	21.4
5<10 ha	11.0	4.4	2.7
> 10 ha	2.4	1.0	0.8
Source: ANE			

There was also a notable difference in the use of farming technology. A much larger percentage of farmers in the South used improved seeds and chemical fertilizer (Table 3). The higher use of pesticides in the Centre and in the North is due to the higher numbers of cotton growers who are usually supplied with pesticides by the outgrower company (Table 3).

Table 3 Farming Practices			
	South (%)	Centre (%)	North (%)
Improved Seeds	25.6	15.2	3.3
Chemical Fertilizer	6.1	1.5	1.5
Pesticides	3.2	4.9	11.2
Source: ANE			

Although households in the South appear to be growing staple crops in at least the same proportions as other regions, the percentage of households in the South selling crops is significantly less than in other regions (Table 4). The 1996 miners' study found that the majority of miners' households were entirely dependent on mine earnings as a source of cash income. The contribution of agricultural sales in the vast majority of cases was negligible. While the national average is 29%, only a small minority of miners' households (11.4%) sell their crops. A large percentage of households in the North are engaged in selling crops because this is virtually the only way households can earn cash. Although the amounts are small, this cash is used for buying basic consumer goods and paying for services such as health and education.

Table 4: Households Growing and Selling Selected Crops						
Crops	South		Centre		North	
	% households growing	% selling (of those growing)	% households growing	% selling (of those growing)	% households growing	% selling (of those growing)
Maize	90	17	83	22	89	70
Manioc	86	19	48	10	72	41
Groundnuts	69	13	26	12	38	51
Sweet Potatoes	45	7	45	11	25	57
Sorghum	2	17	45	5	46	46
Vegetables	60	8	20	32	17	41
Rice	4	32	31	13	28	38
Sesame	23	16	8	12	7	96
Millet	2	0	22	2	3	40
Cotton	2	68	7	82	13	98
Sunflower	1	25	3	26	2	73
Other crops	19	14	14	13	46	30
Cashew	32	16	3	37	16	78
Coconuts	30	18	1	46	6	95
Other fruit	17	27	10	40	17	95
Source: ANE						

Traditionally, the main form of savings for migrants with surplus earnings is livestock, particularly cattle. The civil war which ended in 1992 had decimated the national herd. This is slowly recovering and there are indications that households still attach a great deal of importance to livestock accumulation. Table 5 shows that households of the

South hold significantly more livestock than the other regions, with the greatest disparities arising in relation to cattle ownership.

Table 5: Ownership of Livestock

Type of livestock	South		Centre		North	
	%	Average number	%	Average number	%	Average number
Cattle	18.5	6.4	4.8	7.7	0.1	2.0
Goats	52.7	5.2	38.8	9.3	21.7	6.1
Pigs	42.3	2.9	22.8	4.9	6.3	3.3
Chickens	72.6	11.4	68.1	10.2		8.3
Source: ANE						

In the South, the two dominant non-agricultural activities are (a) the production of traditional drinks and (b) commerce, followed by the production/sale of charcoal and firewood and "specialized" work. In the Centre, commerce is the dominant activity, followed by traditional drinks and then a group of activities that are more or less equal in ranking, including charcoal and firewood, handicraft fishing/selling fish and specialized work. In the North three activities are closely bunched at the top; handicrafts, commerce and charcoal/firewood. In the South between 20-60% of all the homesteads involved in these activities earned at least the equivalent of US $40 per month. By contrast, only about a fifth of the households of the Centre and North involved in commerce managed to earn at this level. Very few households involved in the other activities managed to earn at this level.

Much higher percentages of the households in the South hold commonly owned assets with the exception of bicycles (Table 6).

Households in the South are also much more inclined to make investments than those in the other regions (Table 7). More than half the male-headed households in the South invested more than the equivalent of USD 40 in the previous year compared with considerably lower percentages in the Centre (39.1%) and North (17.7%). Female-headed households tended to invest less but in similar regional proportions as male-headed households. Most of the investment went into construction or renovation of residences. Relatively little went into agricultural activities or transport.

Not only is the proportion of households undertaking investments larger than 500,000 MT significantly greater, the value of the investments were also higher. More than a quarter of the households in the South invested values in excess of 5 million MT (about USD 400) in residences, agricultural equipment, transport and animals. In contrast,

Table 6: Selected Inanimate Asset Holdings

Type	South	Centre	North
Solar panel	17.6	0.6	0.2
Bicycle	35.1	51.7	40.1
Pick-up van	20.0	0.8	0
Car	7.8	0.6	0.1
Tractor	1.9	0.3	0
Refrigerator	14.2	1.5	0
Television	11.7	1.9	0
Video	10.6	0.6	0
Music system	35.9	14.3	3.6
Generator	3.9	0.1	0
Grain mill	12.6	0.6	0.1
Plough	17.6	2.5	0.1
Watch	66.7	34.0	10.1
Water tank	12.8	1.6	0.1
Large water drum	59.1	9.2	2.1
Source: ANE			

Table 7: Investments (above 500,000 MT) made in last year (% of households)

	South	Centre	North
Male-headed	54.1	39.1	17.7
Female-headed	35.4	24.8	10.0
Residence	35.8	16.0	6.7
Transport	6.9	12.0	5.6
Agricultural equipment	4.8	2.7	3.6
Animals	8.6	2.4	1.1
Source: ANE			

virtually none of the investing households of the Centre and North had reached such levels.

The ANE survey also showed that rural households in the South had much better access to social services such as education, health services and roads. Due to the difficulties of measurement and recall, the ANE/Austral survey failed to obtain accurate information on household self-consumption of agricultural produce and livestock.

Notwithstanding, an attempt was made to consolidate numerous variables (including wage income, investments, housing materials, assets, farming techniques, size of farm, and so on) and to convert them (somewhat subjectively) into "wealth points" (see Appendix for details on what variables were selected and their point distribution). As expected, the distribution of wealth points was highly skewed towards poverty with the vast majority of households considered poor. More than three-quarters (77.3%) had less than 50 points and half had less than 25 points (the average being 36.8). Only 5.5% had more than 100.

Levels of wealth vary considerably between the regions. More than half the households in the South were found to be in the highest quartile (Table 8). By contrast, almost half the households of the North were found in the lowest quartile and barely 5% in the highest quartile[14].

Table 8: Distribution of Wealth Points by Region (%)				
Quartiles	Region			Total
	South	Centre	North	
1st quartile (lowest)	11.6	24.4	48.0	26.7
2nd quartile	12.8	27.9	28.9	24.1
3rd quartile	23.7	28.6	17.4	24.6
4th quartile (highest)	51.9	19.1	5.7	24.6
Total	100	100	100	100
Source: ANE				

There is a greater concentration of female-headed households in the lowest quartile. More than a third (35.7%) of female-headed households fall into the lowest quartile compared to just under a quarter of the male-headed households. Somewhat surprisingly, however, amongst the wealthiest households, there appears to be an almost equal chance among female or male-headed households to be in the highest quartile (25.3% for male-headed and 21.6% for female-headed).

REMITTANCES AND POVERTY IN THE SOUTH

In the previous section, inter-regional household welfare comparisons provided convincing evidence that the accumulated effect of both internal and external migration has resulted in a significant disparity of wealth between the households of the South and those of the Centre and North. This section seeks to demonstrate that, although the overall impact of labour migration has been positive in the southern region as a whole, involvement in migrant wage labour itself does not necessarily guarantee that the household will be better off than households that have not sent members abroad to work.

The most obvious cause of economic differentiation between external migrant-sending households would be the level of remuneration which, in turn, depends on the income-generating capacity of the migrant for which level of education and years of experience would be good indicators. The level of remuneration would also be affected by the sector of employment, privilege of certain households in gaining access to the mining sector and the legal status of the migrant. Differentiation is also strongly influenced by the degree of commitment of migrant workers to remit money or goods to their households. This, in turn, is influenced by the facilities available to different types of migrants to remit money or remittances. This differs by type of migrant, location and sector.

Another important factor is the size of the family, which usually determines the labour resources available for migration. In most rural areas a minimum number of members will be needed at home to ensure that basic household needs are undertaken. As the opportunity cost of migration decreases, the incentive to migrate increases for "redundant" household members. Larger households would therefore have a larger propensity to "export" household labour. Closely related to this issue is gender as de jure female-headed households would have a much lower propensity to export labour than male-headed ones.

Finally, a very important determinant of household differentiation is the history of migration of the households. Through primogenitor inheritance and the tendency of many households of the South to continue sending sons to work on the South African mines, those with a multi-generational migrant history are likely to have accumulated more assets (i.e. cattle, land, housing, household goods, vehicles) than those with a shorter history.

This section draws mainly on the findings of the Mozambique component of the MARS survey of external migrant-sending households. Remitted cash is the most frequently cited source of household income (75.5%) followed by remitted goods (64.2%) (Table 9). Income from wage work was cited by a third of the households (33.5%). If "wage income" refers largely to deferred pay, combined with the values attributed to migrant related contributions, migrant contributions provide the overwhelming share of household income (Table 10). Migrant remittances (cash and goods) are therefore used as a proxy for total household income.

Some 78% of the households interviewed have migrants sending money home. Significantly, almost a quarter (22%) of the migrant-sending households do not receive cash income from migrant workers. This percentage may be partly inflated by the fact that some households may not yet have received a cash transfer (as new entrants into the migrant labour system) or the respondent was not aware of cash transfers. It is also likely that many migrants are working under such exploitative

Table 9: Household income from all sources (by frequency)			
	Responses	% of households	% of responses
Wage work	243	33.5	13.6
Casual work	103	14.2	5.8
Remittances – money	548	75.5	30.6
Remittances – goods	466	64.2	26
Income from farm products	161	22.2	9
Income from formal business	30	4.1	1.7
Income from informal business	157	21.6	8.8
Pension/disability	23	3.2	1.3
Gifts	22	3.0	1.2
Other	23	3.2	1.3
Refused to answer	11	1.5	0.6
Don't know	4	0.5	0.2
Total	1791		100
Source: MARS			

Table 10 Household Income by Source and Value			
	No.	Mean	Median
Wage work	149	$1,016.19	$608.70
Casual work	44	$226.67	$65.22
Remittances – money	438	$523.99	$347.83
Remittances – goods	266	$393.79	$217.39
Income from farm products	115	$103.84	$39.13
Income from formal business	8	$779.89	$391.30
Income from informal business	84	$255.72	$130.43
Pension/disability	15	$263.45	$86.96
Gifts	12	$60.94	$26.09
Other income	11	$226.48	$52.17
Total income	579	$936.91	$528.26
Source: MARS			

conditions that they do not have sufficient surpluses to remit.

Table 10 shows that that the average value of remittances received is closely correlated with the frequency that the money is sent. Households receiving remittances on a monthly basis averaged about USD 825 vs USD 123 for those receiving once a year. Most migrants send money home either once a month or once a quarter (Table 11).

Mozambican migrants in South Africa have large discrepancies in

Table 11: Frequency and Value of Money Remittances			
	No.	Mean	Median
Twice or more per month	13	$630.77	$365.22
Once a month	135	$862.39	$782.61
More than twice in 3 months	37	$327.09	$304.35
Once in 3 months	147	$0.02	$326.09
Once every 6 months	68	$201.62	$163.04
Once a year	82	$123.40	$65.22
At end of the contract	4	$240.22	$197.83
Other	67	$494.16	$304.35
Don't know	15	$435.65	$478.26
Source: MARS			

their earnings due to three basic factors: i) the sector in which they are engaged which, in the case of the relatively well-paid mining sector, can be said to be the exclusive privilege of those households with members currently engaged in that sector ii) the education and experience of the migrants and iii) the legal status of the migrant.

The MARS survey showed that Mozambican migrants are employed in a variety of sectors (Table 12). Of the 1,081 migrants, 31.3% were involved in mining, 11.4% in informal activities and 1.4% in agriculture while 16.7% were listed as "other"[15]. Significantly, the sector of 18% of the migrants was unknown. This is not surprising as many migrants do not know what type of work they will be doing before they

Table 12: Sectoral Distribution of External Migrants		
Main work place	No.	%
Factory	67	6.4
Mine	329	31.3
Shop	31	2.9
Office	14	1.3
Government	5	0.5
Informal	120	11.4
Domestic	13	1.2
Farm	15	1.4
Profession	31	2.9
School	5	0.5
Other	230	21.9
Don't know	191	18.2
Source: MARS		

leave. Many of these are likely to end up on the farms of adjacent Mpumalanga Province.

Although information was not gathered in relation to the actual levels of earnings, a few important observations can be made. First, about one-third of the migrants work in the mining sector and would be earning substantially more than those engaged in other sectors. The relatively higher level of earnings for miners is complemented by facilities that make the transfer of wages and goods relatively easier than for other migrants, thus making households with mine migrants generally considerably better off than other households. At the other end of the scale, it is likely that many migrants, for whom no information is available, are likely to be those who have relatively little contact with their households and had no fixed plans for work before migrating. Many of these migrants are likely to be irregular and working under exploitative low-paid work.

What has happened over approximately a 20 year period (1975-1994), is that households with mine migrants became a type of elite among external migrant-sending households. With the abolition of apartheid, new opportunities arose for foreign migrants to penetrate areas of the economy hitherto inaccessible. This allowed for Mozambicans with good education and relevant work experience to work in South Africa for considerably higher salaries than in Mozambique. The South African economy effectively became an extension to Southern Mozambique, offering a broad range of employment and income generating opportunities.

Table 13: Age Distribution of External Migrant Workers		
Age	No.	%
14 and less	0	0
15 to 24	127	11.7
25 to 39	514	47.3
40 to 59	182	16.7
60 and over	12	1.1
Don't know	252	23.2
Source: MARS		

Table 13 shows an almost normal distribution of age of the migrants, suggesting that intake and attrition are fairly balanced. Younger migrants are likely to be earning less than older ones, but younger migrants employed on the mines are likely to be earning more than many of the older migrants working in other sectors.

Apart from sector and legitimacy, earnings capacity is largely

Table 14 Education Levels of External Migrant Workers		
Education	No.	%
None	89	8.2
Primary	770	70.5
Secondary	166	15.2
Diploma	0	0
Degree	0	0
Don't know	67	6.1
Source: MARS		

determined by the level of education and work experience. Table 14 shows that the vast majority (at least 70.5%) of the migrants have only primary education and 8.2% have none at all. With the exception of those employed on the mines, and those with many years of work experience, the poorly educated migrants are likely to be earning relatively low wages. Only 15.2% of the external migrants have achieved secondary education and are likely to be earning comparatively higher wages. The majority of migrants (62.4%) had been working in South Africa for less than ten years (Table 15). However, nearly 20% were long-term migrants of 16 years or more.

Table 15: Years Worked Abroad by External Migrant Workers		
Years	No.	%
1-5	284	31.8
6-10	273	30.6
11-15	167	18.7
16 or more	156	17.5
Don't know	13	1.5
Total	893	100
Source: MARS		

The survey showed distinct differences in the average annual amounts of cash remitted by level of education (Table 16). There is a big difference in the amounts remitted by those with only primary and secondary education, the former sending an average of USD 784 and the latter sending USD 1,072. There was considerable sectoral variation, the most notable being the higher amounts linked to the mines and to what were referred to as "professionals" (Table 16). Remittances coming from the "don't know" category were low (closely in line with informal and domestic employment) and may reflect the fact that these migrants are involved in first time or illegal jobs.

Table 16: Annual Cash Remittances by Level of Education and Sector			
	No.	Mean	Median
a. Education			
None	40	$444.60	$304.35
Primary	424	$426.32	$269.13
Secondary	82	$582.36	$347.83
Don't know	28	$492.45	$428.26
b. Main Work Place			
Factory	37	$390.09	$304.35
Mine	249	$537.22	$434.78
Shop	20	$462.15	$201.09
Office	5	$427.22	$243.48
Government	1	$434.78	$434.78
Informal	48	$312.57	$158.70
Domestic	6	$323.19	$304.35
Farm	5	$241.30	$239.13
Professional categories	16	$842.93	$304.35
School	2	$67.39	$67.39
Other	124	$402.84	$173.91
Don't know	43	$338.52	$152.17

The MARS survey found that overwhelmingly the most common form of remitting either money or goods is taking them back personally or through friends, despite significant changes in transfer technology. The most important changes relate to improved banking facilities for miners using TEBA Bank and the pre-paid delivery services of Kawena Distributors. Kawena, formerly limited to serving mineworkers, now offers facilities in various cities and towns in South Africa to anyone wishing to deliver goods to any accessible household in Southern Mozambique or to one of a large network of warehouses.

With time, more sophisticated transfer mechanisms will be increasingly used by Mozambicans working in South Africa. Illiterate or poorly-educated, as well as undocumented migrants, will probably not have access to or be suspicious of using these methods, thereby exacerbating economic differentiation between the relatively wealthy and the poorer households.

Of major importance to the determination of remittance flows is the degree of commitment by the migrant in remitting wages or goods. Commitment is felt to be closely linked to gender, marital status, age and relationship to the household head.

Annually, household heads send considerably more (USD 1,000) than their sons/daughters (USD 625) or spouses (USD 560) and males send more than females (USD 840 vs. USD 688). As expected, the older the migrant, the higher the remittances. Cash remittances also increased by age, increasing steadily up to the 40-59 cohort (average 14m MT/USD1,112) but decreasing thereafter. Married migrants predictably send home much more money than non-married (almost twice as much).

Table 17: Money sent home: average amount over a year by Migrant Type			
Relationship	No.	Mean	Median
Head	285	$570.31	$417.39
Spouse/partner	26	$316.91	$219.57
Son/ daughter	224	$341.41	$173.91
Father/ mother	3	$628.99	$608.70
Brother/ sister	27	$317.01	$173.91
Grandchild	3	$333.33	$434.78
Son/ daughter-in-law	2	$165.22	$165.22
Nephew/ niece	5	$456.96	$217.39
Other relative	1	$380.43	$380.43
Gender			
Male	553	$457.65	$304.35
Female	23	$374.64	$152.17
Age			
15 to 24	55	$247.57	$152.17
25 to 39	292	$457.21	$304.35
40 to 59	119	$612.53	$434.78
60 and over	9	$472.71	$304.35
Don't know	99	$372.19	$217.39
Marital status			
Unmarried	79	$264.92	$160.87
Married	367	$498.29	$347.83
Cohabiting	109	$474.51	$330.43
Divorced	7	$298.14	$260.87
Separated	3	$236.23	$304.35
Widowed	4	$196.20	$109.78
Don't know	1	$260.87	$260.87
Source: MARS			

The MARS survey found that 42.7% of the households cannot depend on their migrant members in times of need. This is partly due to the fact that one in five migrants cannot be contacted during an emergency. The average amount of cash sent for emergencies was approximately USD 100 while for goods sent it was about USD 50. Almost two-thirds of those who had received assistance felt that the money/goods sent was very important.

Commitment is further manifested by the frequency of visits home. The ANE data shows that in the South, only one-tenth (10.4%) of migrants visit their homes regularly (monthly) while 80.3% of the absentee workers return periodically (but predictably) between 1 month to once a year, with 9.5% seldom returning, if at all. The MARS data (Table 6.1.10) found similar patterns: a majority of the migrants (62.4%) return home at the most twice a year (42.5% visit only once a year) (Table 18). Only 10.7% visit more frequently, while the movements of just over a quarter of the migrants is categorized as "other" of whom many would include migrants with unpredictable visiting patterns, including many migrants who are either undocumented or whose activities/plans are not known.

Table 18: Frequency of Home Visits		
Frequency	No.	%
Twice or more per month	21	2.1
Once a month	23	2.3
More than twice in 3 months	13	1.3
Once in three months	54	5.3
Once every 6 months	177	17.4
Once a year	433	42.5
At end of the contract	25	2.5
Other	274	26.9
Source: SAMP		

The evidence from the MARS survey shows that migrant-sending households have a strong tendency towards inter-generation continuity. Although more investigation is needed, evidence suggests that external (and internal) migration is a deepening phenomenon. More than two-thirds (67.1%) of the households interviewed had migrant parents who had previously worked abroad and 43.6% had grandparents who were external migrant workers. The data suggests that only about one-third of the household members interviewed are first generation migrant-suppliers. Although we do not know what percentage of migrant households have ceased sending migrants, the rate of growth of migrant-sending households is assumed to be positive. Generally, households with more than one generation of migration would have accumulated more wealth than households that have just started sending members to seek work either inside Mozambique or beyond.

HOUSEHOLD DIFFERENTIATION

This section focuses on evidence provided by the MARS survey about household economic differentiation, including: expenditures; the need to borrow and sources of loans; perceptions on the impact of migration; and, most importantly, an analysis of poverty levels among external migrant-sending households.

Household expenditure estimates derived from the MARS survey are at best indicative.[16] Table 19 shows the frequency of the types of expenditures incurred in the previous month. Food was by far the most important (89.3%) followed by fuel (mainly wood and paraffin) (46.6%), transportation (44.5%) and education (43.9%). Other important categories included utilities (of particular importance to urban households), clothes, alcoholic drinks and medical expenses.

In terms of value spent, the largest average amounts were spent on building activities (about USD 150) although relatively few households (13.4%) spent money on this category in the previous month. The second highest expenditure was on food (USD 70) which was also the most frequently cited expenditure. The third highest average value was for special events (USD 50) such as weddings and funerals followed by clothing (USD 55).

Food was by far the most dependent on remittances (77.5% claiming that remittances were "very important"). Remittances were also considered to be "very important" for cattle purchases, school fees, clothing, transport costs, vehicle purchase and maintenance, informal sector trading and farm labour costs. Remittances were felt to be "important" to the survival of the household in a significant majority of cases in relation to food (72.7%), medical treatment (63.6%) and for cash income (74.9%).

The relevance of these findings in relation to household differentiation is that expenditure on food and other basic needs overwhelmingly dominates the budget of external migrant-sending households. Comparatively few households (mainly those with miners and a handful of others with members in higher income jobs) therefore have the capacity to invest in housing, cattle or vehicles.

One of the more interesting findings to come out of the MARS study relates to the borrowing patterns of the respondent households.

Table 19: Monthly Household Expenses			
	No.	% of households	% of responses
Food and groceries	648	89.3	20.4
Housing	5	0.6	0.2
Utilities	291	40.1	9.1
Clothes	262	36.1	8.2
Alcohol	240	32.6	7.5
Medical expenses	229	31.5	7.2
Transportation	323	44.5	10.2
Cigarettes, tobacco, snuff	43	5.9	1.4
Education	319	43.9	10
Entertainment	15	2.1	0.5
Savings	84	11.7	2.6
Fuel	338	46.6	10.6
Farming	82	11.3	2.6
Building	97	13.4	3
Special events	80	11.0	2.5
Gifts	41	5.6	1.3
Other expenses	33	4.5	1
No expenses	8	1.1	0.3
Refused to answer question	43	5.9	1.4
Total	3181		100
Source: MARS			

The need to borrow can be seen as an important indicator of vulnerability. A significant 41.7% of the households said that they borrowed money during the last year. Of those borrowing, half borrowed from family, 36.7% from friends and 2.3% from employers. The main reasons for borrowing money were for the purchase of food (33.2%), health care (21.7%) and funerals (4.6%). Financing companies are hardly present with the exception of a few microfinance operators (with almost no presence in the rural areas and usually lending according to small business needs).

Loans are for the most part used for "survival" issues i.e. food and health. These are typical periodic needs of poor households, especially for those who have to rely on irregular remittances. A big advantage for many remittance-receiving families is that they are probably seen as a lower risk for loans than subsistence households with less reliable cash flows. Schooling and business loans are also quite common and are possibly linked to the household's ability to repay.

In terms of the effect on the household, if more household members migrated for work, a significant minority (40.8%) felt that the household would be better off but a majority (59.2%) of the respondents were less sanguine, feeling that there would either be no difference, they would be worse off or they did not know. Although at face value we cannot conclude very much from the response to this question, it can be inferred that the respondents must to some extent be weighing up the negative effects of losing another member, suggesting that many households may have sent the maximum number of members possible without prejudicial effects on the domestic household economy.

Household economic differentiation can be best highlighted through poverty analysis. A common poverty indicator takes the percentage of food expenditures relative to overall expenditures. The MARS survey found that the average percentage of expenditure devoted to food is 56.7%. "Relatively poor" households were defined as those spending between 60-79% of their total expenditures on food and "extremely poor" as spending between 80-100%. The results show that almost a quarter (24.7%) of the households can be considered to be relatively poor and slightly less (22.4%) extremely poor. These findings should be seen with caution for two reasons. The first is that many households depend to a significant extent on self-produced household consumption that is not measured in the above analysis. This would mean that food "expenditure" is even higher than indicated and that the level of poverty is in fact worse than indicated. On the other hand, the proportion of expenditures devoted to food may have been exaggerated given the fact that most households were interviewed the month following traditionally high consumption periods (Christmas/New Year).

Other indicators suggest a high level of poverty amongst a significant portion of migrant-sending households. The MARS suvery found that 24.1% of the households are often without food and 11.3% are often without medical care. Although these households are very dependent on cash income, 36.8% of the households claim to have often been without cash and 32.6% several times without cash.

Despite the difficulties associated with getting accurate figures relating to the poverty indicators, the data suggests that many of the external migrant sending households are indeed very poor. These findings underscore what earlier work on Mozambique demonstrated i.e. that there is a high degree of economic differentiation among migrant sending households ranging from the elite who benefit from several migrants with relatively high mine wages or professional salaries to households who are forced to send members to work under poor conditions for lack of suitable employment in Mozambique.[17]

CONCLUSION

The rural areas of Southern Mozambique (or the South) have fewer resources and are agriculturally poorer and more vulnerable to climatic instability compared to the rural areas of the Centre and North. Yet, as this study has demonstrated, the pool of economic assets of the average rural household in the South is far greater than for other regions. This disparity can be largely explained by the phenomenon of wage migration. Although a significant number of households in the South have migrant and commuter members working for wages in the domestic economy (mainly in the industrial enclave of Maputo-Matola), the most significant flow of wage-seeking labour has been, and continues to be, to South Africa.

Early migration may have been largely influenced by push factors such as hut tax, chibalo labour (colonial system of forced labour), drought and famine. Later, however, employment in South Africa, particularly the mines, was the preferred income-generating choice of Mozambican men from the rural (and often urban) South. Free transport, board and lodging and a virtually quarantined life, allowed miners to accumulate most of their wages. Compulsory deferred pay (a system of forced savings) further ensured that miners would return to their homes with comparatively large amounts of money and goods. Such remittances were generally used, at least initially, for improving the household's quality of life (through the construction or furnishing of cement-walled homes). Remittances were also used for savings (normally in the form of livestock) or investment. Traditionally, one of the most common investment choices was to buy a pickup (bakkie) for transport purposes (often hired out) or a pump for irrigated agriculture. Now, with the proliferation of vehicles in the rural areas and limited irrigable areas, there is a greater tendency to invest remittances in informal sector trade activities undertaken by resident family members. For many years, import duty exemptions for miners gave further accumulative advantages over other Mozambicans. Although no longer enjoying such privileges, Mozambicans in South Africa can take advantage of distribution services that provide reliable and cost-effective delivery of a large variety of goods direct to their rural base.

Much of Southern Mozambique's external migration history took place during periods when black workers, especially foreigners, were subjected to the most exploitative of conditions. South Africa's migration system was the economic modus operandi of the apartheid system. Yet, despite the degradation and oppression of such work, Mozambican men streamed into South Africa, usually offering a supply much greater than the absorption capacity of a mining industry wary of excessive dependence on one source. Mine work still offered the best of the economic options for the majority of rural work seekers from the South and allowed them to build up their rural home base but at considerable social cost.

Mozambican miners may collectively be seen as a wage elite. Households with several generations of miners are likely to have built up assets and a home-based production capacity that would put them well above the economic status of other households with a more recent involvement in mine-migration. Households with miners with greater skills, longer service or with more than one miner, may have relatively high earnings. However, a significant proportion of mine-sending households could be considered to be poor. Differentiation between households is even more poignant when looked at across the entire range of migrant-sending households. The picture becomes considerably bleaker and suggests that there may be a significant proportion of migrant-sending households that could be worse off because of migration than if the migrant members had stayed at home as the returns to home-based labour might be larger than the contribution derived from the migrant.

Despite Mozambique's economic growth rate being one of the highest in Africa over the past few years, much of the growth is linked to the development of highly capital intensive "mega" projects with limited absorption of unskilled workers. The urban informal sector which has hitherto absorbed considerable numbers of the unemployed has become less attractive for the rural labour surpluses as increasing competition makes economic survival more difficult. Such limitations within the domestic economy, recently exacerbated by the current drought in the South, have forced many rural dwellers to seek employment in South Africa.

The recent agreement between Mozambique and South Africa to abolish visas is an indication of the likely gradual relaxation of the movement of Mozambican wage seekers to South Africa. With limited income-generating opportunities, the implications of more Mozambicans seeking work in South Africa could be greater labour supply and hence a higher likelihood of exploitation. Unlike the mines and some other sectors, Mozambicans engaged in agricultural work or irregular employment are likely to find themselves facing conditions that make regular home visits difficult and the accumulation of savings from very low wages almost impossible. The prospect of a growing number of rural households having to resort to this form of labour migration to South Africa should cause alarm in terms of the Government's current focus on poverty reduction.

Having demonstrated that the overall economic impact of migrant labour has been positive in the South of Mozambique, this paper has also attempted to show that, because the nature of migration has changed so significantly over the last 15 years (i.e. the eclipsing of mine migration and increasing numbers of young Mozambican men chasing a limited number of jobs), it is likely that, in the coming years, the economic impact of migrant labour work in South Africa may diminish quite substantially as the amounts of wages remitted are reduced (due to lower earnings) and the mechanisms available for doing so are much more limited than for miners and workers in other, more privileged, wage sectors.

ANNEX 1. Wealth Point Determinants for ANE Survey		
Determinant	Cohorts	Point Allocation
1. Size of Machamba (fields)	< 1 ha	0
	1-2ha	5
	2-5ha	10
	5 ha +	20
2. Value of crop (000 MT per annum)	<200 (but greater than 0)	1
	200-500	2
	500-1,000	4
	1-2,000	8
	2-5,000	16
	5-10,000	30
	10,000-20,000	40
	>20,000	50
3. Improved Seeds	Yes	10
	No	0
4. Fertilizers	Yes	10
	No	0
5. Pesticides	Yes	10
	No	0
6. Livestock	Per goat owned	1
	Per head of cattle	5
7. Monthly wages (000 MT)	Don't know but > 0	5
	<200	5
	200-500	10
	500-1,000	20
	>1,000	30
8. Monthly Non-Agricultural Income (000 MT)	Don't know but >0	2
	<50	2
	50-100	4
	100-200	8
	200-500	16
	>500	20
9. Animals sold during past 12 months (000MT)	<200	1
	200-500	2
	500-1,000	4
	1,000-2,000	8
	2,000-5,000	16
	5,000-10,000	30

Annex 1 continued

	10,000-20,000	40
	>20,000	50
10. Investments (annual) (MT)	.5-1m	5
	1-3m	10
	3-5m	20
	>5m	30
11. Housing materials	Cement block	40
	Other	0
	Cement/tiled floors	5
	Other categories	0
	Water piped in or out of house/well in yard	10
	Other categories	0
	Electricity supplied	30
	Electricity not supplied	0
12. Other assets	Solar panel	5
	Generator	5
	Water pump	20
	Grain mill	20
	Plough	5
	Refrigerator	5
	Radio	2
	Music system	3
	Television	5
	Video	5
	Watch	1
	Boat	15
	Fishing net	3
	Bicycle	3
	Motor cycle	20
	Pick up van	50
	Car	50
	Truck	80
	Tractor	50
	Water tank	3
	Drums (200 lts)	1
	Other large water containers	1
	Cool box	1

ENDNOTES

1   Simon Katzenellbogen, South Africa and Southern Mozambique: Labour, Railways, and Trade in the Making of a Relationship (Manchester : Manchester University Press, 1982); Alan Jeeves, Migrant Labour in South Africa's Mining Economy: The Struggle for the Goldmines' Labour Supply, 1890-1920 (Montreal and Kingston: McGill Queen's University Press, 1985) and Patrick Harries, Work, Culture and Identity: Migrant Laborers in Mozambique and South Africa, c1860-1910 (Cape Town: David Philip, 1995).

2   Ruth First, Black Gold: The Mozambican Miner, Proletarian and Peasant (New York, 1983).

3   Fion de Vletter, 'Labour Migration to South Africa: The Lifeblood for Southern Mozambique' In David A. McDonald, ed., On Borders: Perspectives on International Migration in Southern Africa (New York: St Martin's Press, 2000), pp. 46-70.

4   Jonathan Crush, 'The Discourse and Dimensions of Irregularity in Post-Apartheid South Africa' International Migration 37 (1999): 125-49; and Lyndith van der Westhuizen, Illegal Migration in South Africa: In the First 10 Years of Democracy, Immigration Advisory Board, Cape Town, 2005.

5   The work was supervised by the author of this paper, so considerable emphasis was placed on aspects of labour migration, an issue that had not been adequately dealt with in most previous household surveys.

6   Data from this survey, in terms of the national currency (metical), has been converted at the rate of 12,500MT = USD 1.

7   Data from this survey, using the national currency (metical), has been converted at the rate of 23,000MT = USD 1.

8   Fion de Vletter, Sons of Mozambique: Mozambican Miners and Post-Apartheid South Africa, Migration Policy Series No. 8, Cape Town, 1998.

9   No comparisons were made with the North as the number of households with wage workers (73) was considered to be too small to be statistically meaningful in comparison with 686 for the South and 982 for the Centre.

10 The term "external migrant" in this study has been applied to anyone who is absent from the household and located in a foreign country for the purposes of earning an income. Under this definition external migrants would include informal traders (hawkers), many of whom go back an forth to neighbouring countries to sell their goods in Mozambique. It also includes self-employed business persons, many of whom have informal activities.

11 Some 49.1% of the household population is considered to be adult (i.e. 20 years or older) and 35.6% of HH population are adults with the categories household heads, spouses, in laws, brothers, etc. This means that 13.5% of the household population (832) are either sons/daughters, grandchildren or nephews/nieces with an age of 20 or above. For simplicity's sake we have

assumed they are all sons/daughters. Further assuming that half are male, we get 416 adult sons. There are 557 sons/daughters who are migrants. There are a total of 75 female migrants. Assuming all come from the son/daughter category, we are left with 482 sons who have migrated. From this we can assume that almost all adult sons have migrated to SA and some daughters. It should be noted that some migrants are likely to be less than 20 years old as 11.7% of migrants are aged between 15-24.

12 During recent interviews with urban households in Maputo, the author was struck by the number of households who were not aware of the work their migrant members were engaged with in South Africa.

13 Census data (1997) show household sizes of approximately 3.8 for the North, 4.5 for the Center and 4.6 for the South. These are consistent with the survey findings since the census includes individuals (i.e. one person households) which accounts for 10.3% of all households, while excluding migrants that have been away for more than 6 months who would be included as residents by the survey respondents.

14 Although there are indeed stark differences between the regions, the wealth point distribution is distorted by fact that self-consumed production is not included. As seen, a poverty analysis based mainly on consumption finds that the Northern region is the best off and the South the worst. Because cash income is a substitute for self-consumption for many households in the South and is relatively easily measured and incorporated in the wealth point calculation, a more realistic depiction would show a downward adjustment for the South and an upward one for the North and Centre.

15 This is likely to be seriously underestimated as many Mozambicans are known to be hired (often illegally) on the farms, mainly in Mpumulanga Province. It is likely that many agricultural workers were listed as "other" or "unknown".

16 It was optimistic to expect poorly educated respondents (many of whom were not involved in the actual expenditures) to recall how much was spent on a long list of possibilities over the previous month. The other influencing issue is that many of the interviews took place in January just after the "festive season" meaning that the "previous month" was December, during which an inordinate amount would have been spent on food and clothing. Other interviews took place in February resulting in January being the previous month during which very little expenditure of any sort would have taken place.

17 First, Black Gold.

MIGRATION POLICY SERIES

1. *Covert Operations: Clandestine Migration, Temporary Work and Immigration Policy in South Africa* (1997) ISBN 1-874864-51-9
2. *Riding the Tiger: Lesotho Miners and Permanent Residence in South Africa* (1997) ISBN 1-874864-52-7
3. *International Migration, Immigrant Entrepreneurs and South Africa's Small Enterprise Economy* (1997) ISBN 1-874864-62-4
4. *Silenced by Nation Building: African Immigrants and Language Policy in the New South Africa* (1998) ISBN 1-874864-64-0
5. *Left Out in the Cold? Housing and Immigration in the New South Africa* (1998) ISBN 1-874864-68-3
6. *Trading Places: Cross-Border Traders and the South African Informal Sector* (1998) ISBN 1-874864-71-3
7. *Challenging Xenophobia: Myth and Realities about Cross-Border Migration in Southern Africa* (1998) ISBN 1-874864-70-5
8. *Sons of Mozambique: Mozambican Miners and Post-Apartheid South Africa* (1998) ISBN 1-874864-78-0
9. *Women on the Move: Gender and Cross-Border Migration to South Africa* (1998) ISBN 1-874864-82-9.
10. *Namibians on South Africa: Attitudes Towards Cross-Border Migration and Immigration Policy* (1998) ISBN 1-874864-84-5.
11. *Building Skills: Cross-Border Migrants and the South African Construction Industry* (1999) ISBN 1-874864-84-5
12. *Immigration & Education: International Students at South African Universities and Technikons* (1999) ISBN 1-874864-89-6
13. *The Lives and Times of African Immigrants in Post-Apartheid South Africa* (1999) ISBN 1-874864-91-8
14. *Still Waiting for the Barbarians: South African Attitudes to Immigrants and Immigration* (1999) ISBN 1-874864-91-8
15. *Undermining Labour: Migrancy and Sub-contracting in the South African Gold Mining Industry* (1999) ISBN 1-874864-91-8
16. *Borderline Farming: Foreign Migrants in South African Commercial Agriculture* (2000) ISBN 1-874864-97-7
17. *Writing Xenophobia: Immigration and the Press in Post-Apartheid South Africa* (2000) ISBN 1-919798-01-3
18. *Losing Our Minds: Skills Migration and the South African Brain Drain* (2000) ISBN 1-919798-03-x
19. *Botswana: Migration Perspectives and Prospects* (2000) ISBN 1-919798-04-8
20. *The Brain Gain: Skilled Migrants and Immigration Policy in Post-Apartheid South Africa* (2000) ISBN 1-919798-14-5
21. *Cross-Border Raiding and Community Conflict in the Lesotho-South African Border Zone* (2001) ISBN 1-919798-16-1

22. *Immigration, Xenophobia and Human Rights in South Africa* (2001) ISBN 1-919798-30-7
23. *Gender and the Brain Drain from South Africa* (2001) ISBN 1-919798-35-8
24. *Spaces of Vulnerability: Migration and HIV/AIDS in South Africa* (2002) ISBN 1-919798-38-2
25. *Zimbabweans Who Move: Perspectives on International Migration in Zimbabwe* (2002) ISBN 1-919798-40-4
26. *The Border Within: The Future of the Lesotho-South African International Boundary* (2002) ISBN 1-919798-41-2
27. *Mobile Namibia: Migration Trends and Attitudes* (2002) ISBN 1-919798-44-7
28. *Changing Attitudes to Immigration and Refugee Policy in Botswana* (2003) ISBN 1-919798-47-1
29. *The New Brain Drain from Zimbabwe* (2003) ISBN 1-919798-48-X
30. *Regionalizing Xenophobia? Citizen Attitudes to Immigration and Refugee Policy in Southern Africa* (2004) ISBN 1-919798-53-6
31. *Migration, Sexuality and HIV/AIDS in Rural South Africa* (2004) ISBN 1-919798-63-3
32. *Swaziland Moves: Perceptions and Patterns of Modern Migration* (2004) ISBN 1-919798-67-6
33. *HIV/AIDS and Children's Migration in Southern Africa* (2004) ISBN 1-919798-70-6
34. *Medical Leave: The Exodus of Health Professionals from Zimbabwe* (2005) ISBN 1-919798-74-9
35. *Degrees of Uncertainty: Students and the Brain Drain in Southern Africa* (2005) ISBN 1-919798-84-6
36. *Restless Minds: South African Students and the Brain Drain* (2005) ISBN 1-919798-82-X
37. *Understanding Press Coverage of Cross-Border Migration in Southern Africa since 2000* (2005) ISBN 1-919798-91-9
38. *Northern Gateway: Cross-Border Migration Between Namibia and Angola* (2005) ISBN 1-919798-92-7
39. *Early Departures: The Emigration Potential of Zimbabwean Students* (2005) ISBN 1-919798-99-4
40. *Migration and Domestic Workers: Worlds of Work, Health and Mobility in Johannesburg* (2005) ISBN 1-920118-02-0
41. *The Quality of Migration Services Delivery in South Africa* (2005) ISBN 1-920118-03-9
42. *States of Vulnerability: The Future Brain Drain of Talent to South Africa* (2006) ISBN 1-920118-07-1

www.ingramcontent.com/pod-product-compliance
Lightning Source LLC
Chambersburg PA
CBHW080428270326
41929CB00018B/3203